INDIANS
ON THE MOVE

INDIANS ON THE MOVE

written and illustrated by
ROBERT HOFSINDE
(GRAY-WOLF)

William Morrow and Company New York

To my friends at William Morrow, especially those with whom I have had close contact over the years. May their moccasins reach the fourth hill of life, that of old age.

I wish to thank the eminent Dr. John C. Ewers, Senior Ethnologist, Smithsonian Institution, for permission to use the description of the travois from his work, *The Horse in Blackfoot Indian Culture,* Bureau of American Ethnology, Bulletin 159.

CONTENTS

1. INDIAN TRAVELS

The Indians of North America were frequently on the move. Some of their travels were migratory, some were due to seasonal activities, and some came about in the course of daily routine.

Early man first came to this continent 30 to 40 thousand years ago across Bering Strait. This trip was a migration. The people were moving their place of abode to a distant locality. As there were no other human beings living here, we know these early immigrants were the ancestors of at least some of the people we today call the American Indians.

Through the centuries that followed, more and more people came and joined together into tribes. The tribes chose leaders and gradually developed their individual cultures. Then the tribes themselves made migratory moves throughout the continent. The Navaho and Apache tribes of the Southwest originally came out of the far northwestern part of Canada 900 or 1000 years ago. By what route they came, or how long their migration took, is still not known, nor do we know why they made the long journey south.

Migrations were frequently caused by one tribe driving another out of a certain territory. It may be that the warlike Cree drove the Navaho and Apache from the North. In the seventeenth century the aggressive pressures of the Sioux Indians forced the Cheyenne to move west, where they settled along the Cheyenne River in present-day North Dakota. In time, as the Sioux moved westward they once again forced the Cheyenne to move. Eventually the Cheyenne were driven down to the Black Hills in South Dakota, and there they lived for several generations. Finally, about 1830, the Cheyenne divided into two bands, the Northern Cheyenne going to Montana, while the Southern Cheyenne moved to Oklahoma. During these migrations the material culture of the former woodland peoples changed to that of the Plains Indians.

Fear of their foes caused the Hopi of the Southwest to move their village from the foothills to the high mesas where they still live today. When they lived among the foothills, they were constantly being raided by the Spaniards, the Navaho, and the Apache.

A misfortune such as an epidemic could cause a whole village to move. When illness, such as smallpox, struck a village killing nearly all the people, those who survived believed that a spirit or demon did not want them living in that place. And so, not to offend the spirit, they packed up and moved away. To be sure that they were well out of reach of the evil spirit, they often traveled for many days before settling down again.

Crop failure caused the Iroquois to move their entire village about every ten or twelve years. They were tillers of the soil, raising corn, squash, beans, and melons in the fields outside their longhouse homes. Having no knowledge of crop rotation, the Iroquois farmers exhausted the soil of its growth minerals. Living for so long in one place also caused a shortage of firewood and building material. Daily the women had to go deeper and deeper into the woods to find what they needed.

When these problems occurred a new village site was chosen. Then the families began moving back and forth between the old and the new village, transferring their belongings. The men took over the construction of the new homes, while the women started the backbreaking task of clearing, tilling, and planting new fields.

The tribes of the plains and woodlands also made

seasonal moves. The Northern Plains Indians moved four times each year. The open prairie where the tribe lived in summer did not provide the shelter needed in cold weather. Early in the winter bands set out to find protected places where there would be water, wood, and grass available. The camps were usually set up in some broad, timbered river valley offering shelter from wind and snow. If enough game could be hunted around the winter camp the people stayed in that place. If not, and if better hunting was to be found in another area, the camp was sometimes moved to that location.

November was the usual time to leave for the winter camp, and when the geese began flying north the people knew the time had come to return to the prairie for the spring hunting season. The bands hunted the buffalo as they moved onto the prairie to set up the summer encampment. During the spring move the women dug prairie turnips and camas, which gave them a welcome change from the meat diet of the winter.

The summer encampment was an orderly affair. Each band set up its lodges at the place designated by the warrior society acting as the tribal police. When all the tribal members finally had arrived, the camp circle was often a mile in circumference. Only the summer camp was laid out in a circular pattern. In other seasons the tepees were usually set up in a line along a stream. With all the people together once again, there was much to talk about, such as tales from the winter camps of newborn babies and of people passing on to the Sand Hills. The summer camp usually stood from early June until the beginning of September. After the sun dance was held at the end of August, the camp circle broke up and the bands separated for the fall buffalo hunt.

During this hunt each family took as many animals as possible so that they would have a good supply of meat for their winter needs. The buffalo meat was cut into thin strips and hung on racks to dry. While the meat was drying, the camp remained in one place for several days. The women gathered berries, which were pounded together with tallow into the meat to form pemmican. Whenever the hunt was successful the camp stayed together longer, but if the buffalo were few in number the people moved the camp and all their belongings.

When the Plains Indians moved they did not travel single file. A line of armed warriors led the march. Following them came the women and children and the old people. They were protected by more warriors walking on either side of them, and the rear of the group was closed in by still other men. The women and older children guided the camp dogs, which pulled baggage. After the coming of the horse this pattern remained the same, except for the difference that nearly everyone rode.

Among many of the woodland tribes the group did not travel as often, and their move into winter camp was not to seek better shelter, which they already had. The woodland tribes moved into winter camp in search of food. In cold weather the deer and moose left the open places to find cover in the heavier timber, and so the woodland people followed the animals deeper into winter hunting areas.

Their winter camps were small, the group usually consisting of a single family of man, wife, and children, though sometimes one or two of the grandparents went along. With the approach of fall the families rolled up their reed mats from the floor area of their wigwams. They took down the mats that covered the inner walls, and these, together with their household utensils, clothing, and personal belongings, were placed in the center of their birchbark canoes. Each woman carried two bundles of firewood on her back for use on the trip. The family dogs, which carried loads around the home and on hunting trips, also went into the canoes. Then, when all preparations were made and after bidding goodbye to relatives and friends, the group was on its way.

Once they reached their hunting area the Indians took little time to establish camp. The framework of the wigwam left in the spring often needed only a new support here and there, and the bark slabs used to cover the structure were close at hand. When the wigwam was set up, the hunt began. Meat was cut up and loaded into bark boxes that were pulled home by the dogs. The average dog could pull a load weighing about thirty pounds. Once the snows covered the ground the dogs were used to pull the hunter's sled.

Tribes such as the Iroquois, Cherokee, and others who lived in permanent villages did not make seasonal trips. Neither did the Indians of the Northwest Coast, nor the Pueblo of the Southwest.

Whether for migration, seasonal trips, or in the ordinary traveling they did in their daily lives, the North American Indians resourcefully devised ways to move themselves and their belongings with speed and efficiency. The equipment they developed and the way they used it are still of interest today.

2. BY FOOT AND HORSE

The American Indian walked over the land for thousands of years. Until the horse came into his life, the Indian traveled with amazing competence under his own power. The distance an Indian could walk in a day depended on the terrain. Under fair conditions he could go twenty to twenty-five miles in one day. In hilly country or over rocky ground the distance would, of course, be less.

One of the reasons an Indian could cover so much ground was the way he walked. The Indian points his toes straight ahead while the average white person toes out. With this angled foot placement the knee tends to turn in its socket and the upper leg bone turns in an awkward position at the hip. These unnatural bone positions cause a person to tire much sooner than if he adopted the Indian walk. When carrying a burden on his back, the Indian sags slightly at the knees with every step. Most white men do not bend their knees, and so they jar their knees at every step.

An Indian walked a sizable distance in a day only when he was traveling alone as a messenger or with a few others as scouts. When the entire tribe was on the move, the people went a much shorter distance. Moving with children and old people took time. A distance of ten or fifteen miles from sunup to midafternoon was a good day's march. The people came to a halt early enough to allow time for the women to set up the tepees before dark. In bad weather or over rough ground the distance was often not more than five miles a day.

The single, or Indian file, style of walking was common among the woodland tribes and among those living in the mountains. Woodland trails rarely measured more than eighteen inches wide, and they seldom ran in a straight line. Leading in all directions, the numerous paths crossed and recrossed each other, much like the roads shown on our modern road maps. New trails were often made when spring and fall storms blew down many trees. When the Indian could go under or over such windfalls, he did so, but if the trail was blocked completely, he had to go around them.

In places where an enemy might be encountered, the Indian walked especially carefully. He avoided dry grass that would break underfoot, revealing the direction he had gone. He also avoided stepping on dry twigs that would snap, and he tried not to step on soft or bare ground where his moccasins would leave a mark.

Many people think that an Indian could walk through the forest in complete silence. That belief is not quite true. His soft-soled moccasins did help to silence his steps, and where the forest floor was covered with a carpet of dead pine needles, he could not be heard. Walking on a cover of dry leaves was quite another matter. Then he was as hard pressed to walk in silence as any other person. Only in the morning when the leaves were moist with dew or when they were wet from a rainstorm could he walk on them quietly.

The Indians were also good runners, and an outstanding runner was held in great respect by his tribe. Among the Iroquois, runners were needed to take certain wampum belts from village to village when war was declared. In the Southwest the ancient Hopi, forebears of the Pueblo of today, hunted rabbits by running them toward a screen of netting set up on the open ground. This method was also used to round up antelope and wild turkeys.

Many of the Indians' prayers for rain—ever important for their fields—involved ceremonial runners. For many centuries the Hopi sent a runner to bring rain. Making a wide circle over the desert, the runner would cover twenty to thirty miles in a day, and if the rain gods favored him, rain and rain clouds would follow in his wake as he returned to the village.

Although the Hopi long ago moved to the high mesas, their fields are still located in the valley below. It is not uncommon, even today, to see an elderly Hopi jog-trot fifteen or so miles to his fields, work there all day, and then trot back home again in the evening. With the same kind of endurance the Penobscot Indians of Maine are known to have hunted deer by chasing them on foot. The men could not run faster than the deer, but eventually they wore the animals down.

As he walked across the land through the years, the Indian left trails that showed the imprint of bare feet, of sandals, and of moccasins. The Indians living along the shores of the two oceans usually went barefooted since much of their lives was spent near or in the water. In the Southwest the heat of the desert sands forced the Indians there to devise protection for their feet. The earliest-known footwear from that region consisted of sandals woven from shredded sagebrush. Archeologists have unearthed samples of such footwear estimated to be over 9000 years old. Such sandals were later replaced by a longer-lasting type of moccasin with a high top and a molded rawhide sole. This moccasin is still being worn today by the Navaho, Pueblo, and Apache.

Moccasins with a buckskin upper and a thin, flat sole of rawhide were prevalent among the Plains Indians. However, a type of soft-soled moccasin was also used by some of the Western tribes. This style was made from one piece of buckskin, part of which formed the sole, the other part the upper. To hold the parts together a seam ran along the outer edge of the foot.

Soft-soled moccasins were also worn by the woodland tribes, and among them the pattern varied from tribe to tribe. Those of the Ojibwa people had the buckskin cradling the foot, with a smaller, U-shaped piece fitted over the instep and sewed in a puckered fashion. Iroquois and Cree moccasins were made from a single piece of skin meeting over the center of the foot, where it was stitched together.

All the walking and running over rough terrain that Indians did was hard on their moccasins, and whenever a man started out on an extended trip he carried several extra pairs with him. Some he put in his pack, but he also tied a few pairs to his belt in

case he had an encounter with an enemy and lost his
pack.

Having been pedestrians for thousands of years, it is surprising how quickly the Indians learned to ride when horses became available. The first Indians to have horses were the Navaho and Apache, since they met the Spaniards first. Little by little horses reached other tribes, either by trade or through raids, and eventually they spread across the country. The Indians of the Northern plains were among the last to obtain them, especially in large numbers.

The Indians learned to ride not only quickly, but remarkably well. Early cavalry officers who fought in the Indian wars have stated that the Sioux and Cheyenne were among the finest horsemen anywhere in the world.

When the Indians first obtained horses, they rode them bareback. In time, for their own comfort, saddles of sorts came into use. The pad saddle was a type used by active warriors. Actually, it was little more than a large stuffed pillow, made from two pieces of skin cut to the same size. A woman stitched the pieces together, lengthwise down the middle. Then she began sewing the edges together, and as she did so, gradually stuffed the sewed part with buffalo wool or deer hair, although some saddles were filled with dry grass. This pad saddle was a man's saddle, rarely used by children, old men, or women.

The women's saddle was known as a frame saddle. Its sideboards were made from two pieces of split cottonwood. The cantle and pommel were fashioned from two forks of green cottonwood, carefully selected for shape as well as for equal size.

Holes were drilled in the forks and through the sideboards, and the parts were laced together with wet rawhide. A small peg of wood was inserted in a hole burned into the front of the fork used as the pommel. The peg quickly identified the front from the back, and it was also a place from which to hang a riding quirt. When the four sections were completed, the entire saddle was covered with wet rawhide, which, as it dried, further helped to hold the saddle together.

To prevent the sideboards from hurting the horse, soft skin pads, stuffed with grass, were tied to the saddle's underside. To protect the rider from the hard sideboards, the saddle was covered with a large, double fold of buffalo skin with the hair left on. Among the different tribes one finds some variations in the style of the frame saddle as well as in the fine saddle ornaments that came into use at a later date.

The prairie-chicken-snare saddle was an all-purpose saddle with the sideboards described above, but with a much lower pommel and cantle, made from elk or deer antler rather than wood. This saddle was used as a riding saddle by the younger men in preference to the pad saddle, and older men, children, and sometimes women used it too. It also served as a pack saddle when moving camp. All saddles used for riding were fitted with rawhide-covered wooden stirrups, and with girth straps and tie rings.

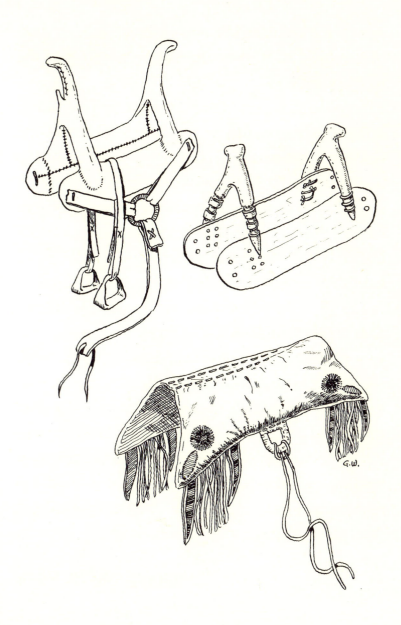

3. TRAVEL BY WATER

A look at a map of the United States and Canada shows an abundance of lakes and rivers. Some of the lakes are large, some small. Some rivers are long while others are short, often being forks extending out from the main rivers like the branches of a tree. This great water system, especially in the eastern half of the United States, was of major importance to the Indian tribes.

Since water is as essential to man as food, tribes built their permanent villages or set up temporary camps along streams. Each morning the Indians bathed before starting the day. Even the smaller children were carried into the water by their elders. After an Indian had purified himself in the sweat lodge, he plunged into the cold waters nearby, and many were good swimmers. As time passed the Indians found ways to travel on these waters, exploring far and wide, and occasionally finding other tribes living miles away on the same river.

The narrow land trails were good enough as hunting or war trails, but as the nomadic tribes grew in numbers, backpacking their belongings through the forests became more difficult. Low-hanging branches got in the way. Exposed roots tripped the travelers, and the long, crooked trails themselves slowed their progress. The open waterways began to seem an attractive alternative route. Perhaps the first experiment was made by someone floating downstream astride a log. The next step was probably the construction of a raft. By lashing several logs together the Indian now had a platform on which he could stand. His feet were no longer in the cold water, and the raft also held some of his belongings or the game he brought back to camp. Moving the raft with the current was relatively easy, but poling the blunt, square-ended platform upstream was quite another matter.

To make the logs for the raft more or less uniform in length, the Indian had to burn one end of some of them, chipping off the charred parts with his bone

or stone tools. From this process he may have come upon the idea that fire, if controlled, could be used to hollow out his log. Experimenting with this technique produced the dugout.

In time, he also discovered that by rounding off the front end of the log, and curving it as well, the log moved more freely in the water. Growing trees were not cut down for dugouts. Windfallen, well-seasoned logs were preferred. Once a suitable one was found, the Indian, with the help of friends, placed it across two smaller logs before work began. Slowly and patiently he chipped away layer after layer along the top and sides of the log, leaving the underside naturally rounded.

Then, to determine the thickness of the dugout's bottom, the builder rolled the log over and drilled several holes into it to a depth of about two inches. The holes were made with a bow drill to which was fitted a sharp point of flint or bone. Alongside the log the Indian built a fire of hardwood, and after the log had been turned right side up again, he placed a layer of hot coals along a section of the flat top. Throughout this burning he took much care to keep the coals away from the outer edges so an even thickness would remain.

After a layer of wood had been burned, the charred parts were chipped away until fresh wood was exposed. This new wood was then left to season for a day or two after which the burning process was repeated. As the burning went deeper and deeper two blocklike sections were left untouched within the log. Extending crosswise near the ends of the log,

these sections served as spreaders as well as seats.

Finally, after much burning and chipping, the holes drilled into the bottom were exposed. At this point the burning ended, and the final touches were added. All traces of charred wood were now chipped away until the inside showed only clean wood. The holes were plugged with wooden rods pounded into place, and when the dugout was put in the water the plugs swelled, making the log watertight. To keep the dugout from becoming waterlogged during prolonged use, the Indian covered it outside with a generous amount of animal fat.

These dugouts were too hard to paddle, so they were poled up and downstream, with the poler standing in the stern. So expert did some of the Indians become in the art of making dugouts that, although they worked entirely by eye-measure, their craft floated evenly. Some of the early Indians using this type of craft were the tribes of Massachusetts, the Cherokee of North Carolina, and the Pequot people along the Mystic River in Connecticut.

TRAVEL BY WATER

In the mid-Atlantic areas the tulip poplar was used for dugouts. When it is green this wood is very heavy, but after it becomes well seasoned it is quite light. South of the James River in Virginia, as well as in Florida, swamp cypress was used. Since the tree grows in water it is well suited for these craft, and the Seminoles made a long, slender, and very graceful dugout with a high pointed prow and a rounded stern.

The Indians along the Northwest Coast carried the art of making dugouts much further than any other tribe. Their craft were actually dugout boats, or canoes, varying in size, shape, and design. Throughout this coastal area the large white cedars were used, and some of the larger dugouts made by the Nootka and Haida were more than sixty feet long and eight feet wide amidship.

These people did not use the burning process. Instead the hollowing out of the straight-grained logs was done by chipping and gouging out the inside with stone, bone, hardwood, and jade blades set into wooden handles. A cross section of the Haida canoe would show its shape to be that of a broad U, whereas the Nootka craft had a flat bottom and straight sidewalls, flaring slightly outward along the upper edges.

A giant cedar was cut down when a craft was to be made, and work on it usually started in the fall. With chisel and maul the Indian roughly shaped the outside and gouged out the inner core. The final work on the inside he completed with a hand adz.

Then came the job of spreading the sidewalls. First he filled the hull with water into which he dropped white-hot stones. As more and more stones were added, the water in time began to heat up and finally to boil. The hot water, and the steam it created, soaked right into the raw wood, and the men could spread the soft sides into the desired shape by pounding in wood spreaders. The spreaders were flat boards, and they were left in place to serve as seats for the paddlers later on.

To make these large craft more seaworthy, the Haida added high ends to both stem and stern.

These additions were constructed from extra pieces of wood, fitted to the ends by means of a zig-zag surface, called a scarf joint. Holes were drilled through the upper edges of the canoe, and the lower edges of the piece to be added, and through these holes the sections were lashed in place with twisted strands of the inner bark of the cedar. Each piece was highly decorated with colorful designs depicting totemic figures of birds and animals. To prevent the craft from becoming waterlogged, the outside was charred by burning the surface with flames from a torch, after which the sides were rubbed thoroughly with fish oil.

These Northwest Indian canoes were made for ocean use in warfare, as well as for trips to visit neighboring tribes. Smaller craft were made for river travel, but were patterned after the larger canoes.

Artists like to paint Indians in bark canoes, and although the dugout canoe was used by far more tribes, the birchbark canoe is certainly more picturesque.

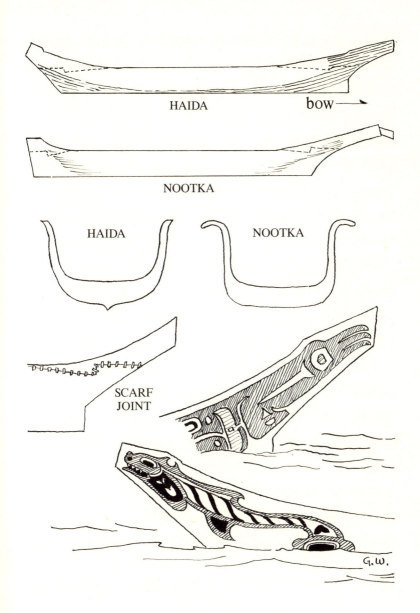

HAIDA

bow →

NOOTKA

HAIDA

NOOTKA

SCARF
JOINT

G.W.

The large paper birch, or canoe birch as it is also called, did not grow below the southern tip of Lake Michigan and extended across the country only from Maine through upper Minnesota. In addition, it grew in Canada. This area of the continent contains many lakes and rivers that flow together to make extensive waterways. The birchbark canoe, being light and durable, offered an ideal means to travel these waters.

Making a canoe of birch bark required time and great skill, but a well-made canoe gave the owner a full year of long trips. When the canoe became old and patched, it was kept at home and used only for short trips near the village or wigwam.

Straight-grained white cedar was the wood most often used for making the canoe frame and paddles. The cedar was split and whittled into the proper sizes for ribs, sheathing, spreaders, and gunwales. Then these pieces were soaked in the river until they became flexible.

Measurements used in the building of the frame

corresponded with distances between parts of a man's body. The depth amidship equaled the distance between the elbow and thumb, and the space between the canoe ribs was the span of a hand from thumb to little finger.

The actual building took place in a shady spot or on cloudy days since the sun would have dried out the wood too quickly. The bark for the covering was collected late in June, a time when it was easiest to remove. If possible it was taken off the tree in one piece. To obtain bark in a single piece, the Indian cut one ring around the base of the tree and another up as high as was needed. Then he cut a straight, vertical slit between them. After a day or two, he could remove the bark between the cuts.

In cases where the bark had not been obtained in a single piece, two or three sections had to be used, overlapping at the edges, which were covered with spruce gum and stitched together with strands of spruce root.

In the swift rivers of the Northeast, falls and rock-

strewn white water sometimes made passage impossible. Then the bark canoe could be portaged to calm waters. The craft was light enough so that an Indian on a hunting trip could easily carry his weapons, small pack, and the canoe itself over a narrow footpath in one trip.

In size the canoes varied from the small river canoes that were paddled by one or two people, to the thirty-five- or forty-foot-long Montreal canoes that were so much favored by the early *voyageurs* of the fur trade. These large canoes were used for travel on the Great Lakes, manned by eight or ten men, and they carried large bales of furs and supplies, as well as trade goods. Once the lake crossings had been completed, the loads were transferred to smaller canoes, known as north canoes, for the final trip over rivers and small lakes to the trading posts. The north canoe measured twenty-four feet in length and carried a crew of four or five men plus a large load.

The canoes of the tribes differed primarily in the shape of the stem and stern. The canoe of the Chip-

pewa, or Ojibwa, Indians compares closely to the modern-day canoe, which is also low in profile. The Slave Indians in the Northwest Territory of Canada favored a canoe with very high ends, much like those of the Montreal canoe. The Interior Salish of British Columbia and Alberta used a canoe whose stem and stern were made in a straight, downward slanting line that brought the pointed ends well under water.

The area now called Newfoundland was the home of the Naskapi Indians. Their canoes were commonly known as crooked canoes. When building one, the ends of the frame were placed on two large boulders, while the center of the frame rested on the ground. This technique raised the stem and stern so that they stayed out of the water, which was an advantage when passing through rapids and foaming white water.

The Iroquois of Canada and the United States made canoes copied from those of their Algonquian neighbors, but the resulting craft were ugly as well as heavy. In place of birchbark, which the Iroquois

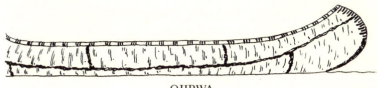

OJIBWA

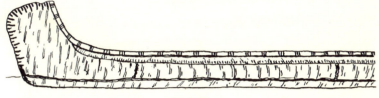

SLAVE

INTERIOR SALISH

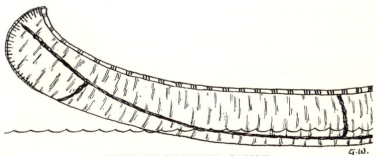

NASKAPI CROOKED CANOE

did not have, they used the rough bark from the elm. The bark was placed on the frame, rough side out, and then scraped to make it smooth. The ends of these canoes did not round in the usual graceful curves, but were straight. Where the bark covering came together at the end it was held in place with two strips of wood lashed together.

The Plains Indians used neither canoe nor dugout. In fact, they traveled very little by water. There were times, though, when rivers had to be crossed, and if they were too deep to ford, the Indians constructed a basket-shaped craft, generally called a bull boat. A large, basketlike frame was constructed from willow branches. Over the outside of this frame the Indians stretched a green, or untanned, buffalo hide and lashed its edges to the upper rim of the frame. This hide was usually that of a buffalo bull, which eventually gave the craft its name.

Belongings, children, women, and older people were ferried across the river in these hide boats. Either the boat was paddled with a flat board, or a

man on horseback towed the bull boat behind him
with a long rawhide rope.

The Mandan Indians always built their permanent
earth lodges near the edge of a river and kept a few
bull boats in the village for frequent crossings. After
use, the bull boat was dismantled, the frame left on
shore, and the hide rolled up and taken along on the
journey.

4. WINTER TRAVEL

An old Indian proverb says: It is not good to travel far when the pony wears his hair long. The time referred to, of course, was winter, when the horses grew a protective layer of hair. The difficult conditions in the cold months of the year forced the American Indians to devise ingenious equipment to make travel possible.

During the winter months the Plains Indians did

not travel far, but stayed close to their tepees in their winter encampments, letting the snow pile up in a protective layer around the lodges. The Northern and Northeastern Indians were more adventurous. The use of snowshoes, sleds, and sled dogs made it possible for them to move about more freely to hunt and set out traps for fur-bearing animals.

Snowshoes were the basic winter apparatus of the Indians. They were made in different styles, depending upon where they were to be used. The snowshoes of the Ojibwa people were typical. They made two types of long snowshoes. One had a rounded front, that curved slightly upward. This model was for woods travel. The other snowshoe had pointed ends front and back. This snowshoe was flat and was used for travel in open country.

Among these people the women had a snowshoe of their own. This style, the so-called bear-paw snowshoe, derived its name from its shape, as well as from the track it left. The shape of the shoe was oval, being slightly longer than it was wide.

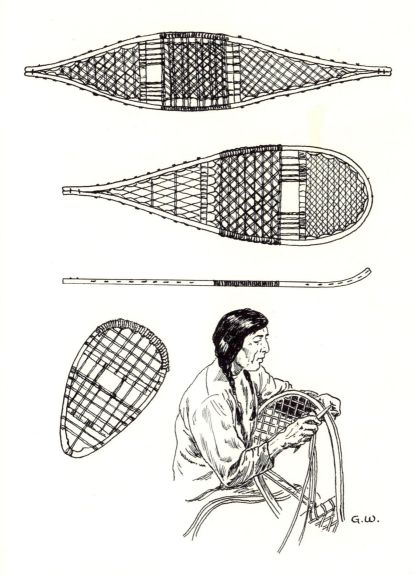

The frames for these snowshoes were cut from green ash. First the wood was made pliable by heating it over a fire or steaming it. After the heat softened the sap, the wood could be bent to the desired shape.

The wood was then shaved down with the ever-handy crooked knife. Originally these knives were made from a beaver tooth. The cutting tooth of that animal has a natural curve and a sharp edge. Years later the Indians made their crooked knives of steel, often from a file. The lower end of these knife blades curves up like a letter J, and they were used in much of the Indians' work with wood.

When the wood was pliable and had been shaved down, pegs were set into the ground in the desired form of the frame, and the wood strips placed within these pegs to dry out. The longer snowshoes had two crosspieces, or spreaders, at either end. The bear-paw had one at the center and one at the rear.

The webbing for snowshoes was made from strips of a moose or deer hide. Moose hide was preferred since it did not stretch when wet or shrink while drying. The webbing used between the toe and the front spreader, and from the back spreader to the heel, was made of thin strips of hide. The webbing across the middle of the shoe was heavier.

To hold the front and back webbing, the Indians drilled holes in pairs in the snowshoe frame. Through them rawhide strips were passed so that they formed a row of small loops on the inner side, and through these the webbing was laced.

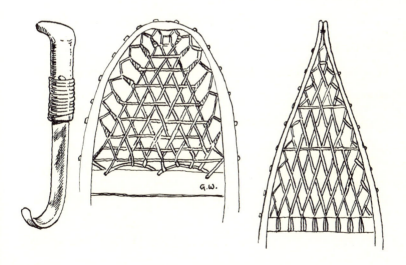

The thicker strips in the middle of the shoe were looped around the frame as the work progressed. To prevent these strips from wearing against the wood, the frame was often wrapped first with a piece of buckskin. In later years red flannel was used. It served the same purpose, while it also added a bit of bright color.

Near the center of the front spreader an opening was left in the heavier webbing through which the toes of the wearer dipped as he walked. A foot length

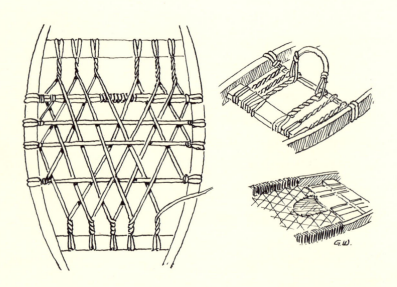

in back of this opening a piece of leather was often laced in place to prevent further wear where the heel came to rest. The foot harness consisted of a single loop, just back of the toe opening, through which the front of the foot was inserted, leaving the heel free.

For the lacing, long strips of hide, all in one piece and of uniform thickness, were needed. The Indians used a special technique to cut them. Setting the point of a sharp knife firmly into a log, or a flat board, with the cutting edge facing forward, the Indian pulled a large, oval piece of hide toward himself. By guiding the hide carefully, he was able to cut long strips in an ever-decreasing spiral.

Although the bear-paw was a woman's snowshoe, a hunter, caught in an unexpected snowstorm, sometimes made a pair from materials close at hand. Using green saplings that bent readily, he shaved down the heel ends with his knife. He bent the frame until it overlapped at the broad toe section. This overlap was lashed together with strips of inner bark from the slippery elm. The webbing and the harness were made from basswood bark.

Wet, slushy snow has a tendency to clog the webbing on ordinary showshoes, so for travel in such conditions the Indians made a snowshoe from a flat piece of wood. Some of these snowshoes were quite narrow and were made from a single board split from a log. The front end was rounded, and the heel tapered. Then in the proper place a hole was cut for the toe opening and the harness added. One finished shoe served as the pattern for the second.

The Naskapi Indians of Canada made a different snowshoe from wood. In shape it resembled the bearpaw, but was wider and somewhat longer. Two boards were used for each shoe. Where they fitted together the edges were left straight, but the toe, sides, and heel were trimmed to a curved shape. The straight edges were lashed together, and two thin strips of wood were lashed across the shoe to make it firm.

* * *

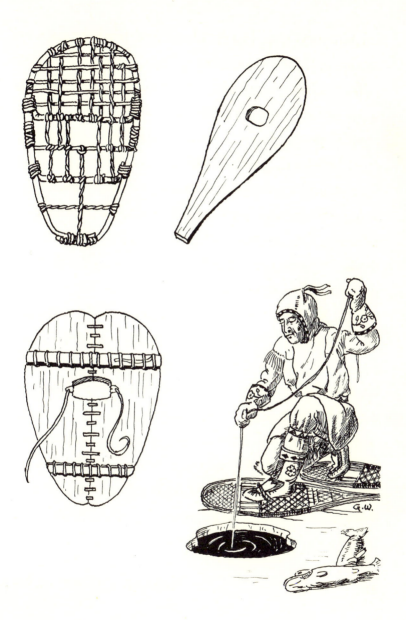

Toboggans and sleds were next in importance to snowshoes. The earliest, and therefore the most primitive of the toboggans, was probably the one used by the Iroquois for pulling loads too large to carry. This toboggan was nothing more than a wide slab of elm bark. The ends were soaked in boiling water to soften them, and then they were folded back upon themselves and held in place with long stitches of spruce-root fibers. The front end was curved slightly upward, and a long pull rope was inserted under the fold.

Such bark toboggans were also used by the children for sliding down snow-covered hills. For this use the bark slab was left wide at the rear end. The front section was trimmed to a long taper and bent upward and inward to serve the child as a handhold. Starting at the top of the hill, the youngster placed one foot on the slab, pushing off with the other foot. Once momentum had been gained he placed both feet together and coasted merrily down the hill.

This bark toboggan may possibly have been the

forerunner of the better and more serviceable one made at a later date from thin birchwood planks. The plank toboggan was the best conveyance developed by the Indians for winter travel, and its use extended far into the northern sections of Canada. The woodland Indians made theirs from two birchwood boards that had been split from a log.

The boards were smoothed as much as possible with the aid of the crooked knife. Then one end of each board was soaked in boiling water and gradually bent up and over until it formed a graceful curve. Next the outer edges were trimmed down. The curved end was eight to ten inches wide, and the tail end about twelve inches wide. The broadest part of the toboggan, a little forward of center, spanned fourteen to eighteen inches. The average length of these toboggans was eight feet.

The two boards were held together with five to six cross-strips of wood, lashed on with rawhide. The ends of each crossbar also had holes cut through them, or they were notched on the underside.

Through the holes long thongs of rawhide were passed loosely so that they formed a row of loops. When a toboggan was loaded, the lashings holding the load passed through these loops, holding the load in place.

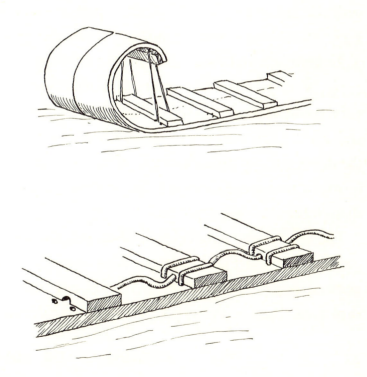

To prevent the curved front from warping after being wet, rawhide cords were fastened to the ends of the front cross-strip and secured tightly to the cross-strip below. Long traces for pulling the toboggan were also fastened to this lower strip.

The plank toboggans were light and resilient and could withstand severe shocks. The curved front made it possible to drag them across most obstacles.

They were, and are today, mostly pulled by a person wearing snowshoes, although in open country two to three dogs, pulling single file, could be hitched to them. The woodland Cree in Canada added a light, upright frame to some of their toboggans, covering it with skins as a protection for a passenger or to shield a load of skins. This style of toboggan, pulled by dogs, was called a cariole by the French Canadians.

The Cree, like most other Indians, are artistic, and their artistry showed on the carioles as well as on the harnesses worn by the dogs. Brightly colored pom-poms, made out of red, green, white, and yel-

low wool yarn, were fastened along the upper rim of the frame, and the dog harnesses had some very colorful blankets added to them. The blankets were made out of wool yarn and velvet cloth obtained from the Hudson's Bay trading posts. Usually they were black and dark blue velvet, and the edges were trimmed with a thick wool fringe containing all the colors found in the pom-poms. A floral design, worked in beads, wool, or dyed moosehairs, or in a combination of all three, was embroidered on the

blanket for added decoration. Small harness bells were often fastened to the blanket, and to add still more beauty a thin strip of wood, bent into an arch, was set up over the dog's shoulders. From the top center of this arch was suspended a large, colorful pom-pom.

Besides toboggans, many tribes also made sleds of various designs, to serve different purposes. The Ojibwa people made a hunting sled for daily use in their winter camps. Although the design was simple, the sled was made with a great deal of care.

Long, slender ash trees were used for the runners, which curved back at the front and continued, all in one piece, as a top pole. A section in the middle of the long ash poles was shaved down slightly, and then soaked in hot water so that the pole could be bent evenly into a curve.

Next, three holes were drilled through each top piece, and directly below them three holes were drilled into the upper side of the runners. These lower holes were drilled only part way into the wood.

Straight pieces of wood, of uniform size, were then cut and the ends trimmed down to the size of the holes in the long poles. The pieces were cut long enough so that the ends would extend slightly through the holes on the top poles after they had been inserted.

Starting near the curved front, the first pair of these uprights were set in place, and a flat board was fitted over the extending pegs on top. The pieces were then lashed together. The other uprights were set in place and lashed in the same manner.

A rough copy of this hunting sled could be made in a short time on the trail if the need arose. The sled had similar lines, but the method of construction differed. Green ash saplings were used and were bent to the shape described above, but without the aid of boiling water.

The uprights were trimmed and placed into holes made in the runners, but the top ends were split and folded back under the top pole. The crosspieces were also split at both ends, and the tops of the uprights

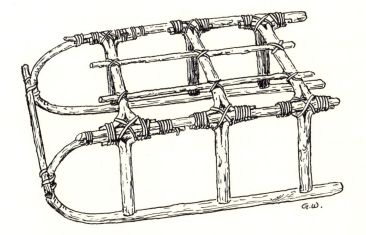

G.W.

and the ends of the crosspieces were lashed to the top pole at the same time. Rawhide or strips of inner bark of cedar or ironwood was used for lashings.

For cross-country travel the Indians made a more complicated sled that required greater skill to construct. It had a platform raised above the runners, side rails, and long handlebars, and was constructed from the elastic green ash, or hickory wood.

The runners and side rails of the open-country sled were made from green saplings. Pairs of pegs were driven into the ground in the pattern desired, and the peeled saplings were fitted between the pegs. They were left to season and dry into the proper shape.

During this drying period the eight uprights, the crosspieces, and the floorboards were cut and shaped. When the runners and the side rails had dried in their molds, notches were cut near the tops of the curved runners. The ends of the hand and floor rails were tapered to fit these notches, and they were lashed in place there. The uprights were lashed to the runners and handrails. Spreaders, lashed between the uprights, supported the floor rails as well as the flat floorboards.

This open-country sled was used where the snow was hard packed. Since the Indian did not have to break a trail for his dogs, he could place both feet on the ends of the runners and support himself by gripping the handrails.

Dogs were usually hitched to these sleds in a fan shape, although they were also used in pairs and in

single file. In the fan-shape hitch, the pulling traces varied in length from fifteen to thirty feet. Each trace was fastened with a set of bone, or wood, toggles to a pull loop attached to the front of a runner.

Usually three dogs pulled at each side with a lead dog well out in front, on the longest trace. Toward the side, the traces became shorter. The harness for each dog was made from a double loop of skin. The loops were crossed where they came to rest on the chest of the dog. The harness was held together across the shoulder with an adjustable strap.

For forest travel the fan-shape hitch was awkward, so the Indians used the single-file hitch instead. A

padded collar was fitted over the neck of the dog and rested on the dog's shoulders. To this collar the pulling traces were fastened and held in place by a simple cinch strap fitted around the dog's middle. The Indians' toboggans were usually pulled by four or five dogs in the single-file hitch.

When well fed, a good dog team could travel fifty or sixty miles in a day, pulling a load of five hundred pounds.

5. THE TRIBE ON THE MOVE

The tribe was moving across the plains once again. It was early fall, and the people had to hunt the buffalo if they were to have enough meat to store away for the long winter ahead.

The day before the move the head chief called a meeting of the different band chiefs and the headmen from four of the men's societies. After discussing the trip with them, he assigned the members of the societies their places during the move. One society was to scout ahead of the people, while the men of the second and third groups were to protect the ranks of the moving column, one on the left, one on the right. The fourth and last group were to remain at the campsite until all the people were on the move. Then they were to follow, guarding the rear.

Once these plans were made, the village herald rode through the camp calling out the news of the coming journey. Now the people began their preparations. All belongings, except for the few articles needed for the night and the morning meal, were packed.

Most of the Plains Indians had special customs concerning the moving of the medicine pipe. In each tribe there was one man who was the custodian of the pipe, which actually belonged to the entire tribe. On the morning of the move, when his lodge was being taken down, the place where the pipe rested told a story. If the Indian placed the pipe bundle, hanging from its tripod, some distance from his tepee, the move was to be a long one taking several days. If he left the bundle displayed close to his lodge, the trip was to be a short one. The pipe stem was tied to the outside skin wrapping of the bundle, and the owner placed it so that the mouthpiece pointed in the direction to be followed. Before the tribe started to move, the pipe custodian made a smudge from sweet grass and offered a prayer for a safe journey for all.

The actual packing by each family was the responsibility of the women, young and old, and each article had its assigned place. So expert were the women in this work that after the morning meal was over they could be completely ready to move in less than one hour.

The lodge cover was folded neatly in a prescribed way and placed across a saddle. Lodge poles were divided up into two equal-size bundles and tied onto either side of a horse. To keep the poles hitched firmly, a small hole was drilled, or burned, toward the top of each pole. Through the holes a rawhide

line was passed, tying the bundle together. Then a connecting line, which held them in place, was run over the lodge cover from one bundle to the other.

Food, such as dried meat, pemmican, and tallow, was packed in flat parfleche cases, suspended in pairs from the sides of one of the packhorses. Pemmican to be eaten for lunch during the march was carried in rectangular parfleche cases hung from the horn of the woman's saddle. Then the tribe got under way, the Indian who was custodian of the medicine pipe led the main group of people.

The Indians moved their belongings on travois pulled by dogs or horses. For many years dogs were the Indian's beasts of burden. The travois they pulled, an A-shaped device, consisted of two poles, crossed near their thinner ends and resting across the shoulders of the dog. Between the spreading poles a platform was placed to hold the load. These platforms were either in the shape of a small ladder or were made from a willow hoop with a netting of thongs. A large dog could drag a sixty-pound load.

The dogs were half-wild, half-domesticated animals, and sometimes a fight would flare up among them, causing the travois to be upset.

Parfleche cases and bags containing the family's ceremonial clothing were carried by some dogs, while still more dogs carried the household goods. Two dogs pulled the tepee poles. In those early, pre-horse days, the lodges were much smaller and the poles shorter than they later became. At first the average lodge was made from six or seven buffalo skins. Later tepees were constructed from twelve to fourteen skins. They weighed about one hundred pounds and had poles weighing twenty pounds each. An average family owned about twenty dogs, and when moving camp all the dogs were employed.

When the Indians obtained horses, they began to use these animals to move their belongings. Well-to-do families often used as many as twelve horses when moving camp, including two riding horses for the men, and two trained buffalo-running horses. Extra horses owned by individual families, and not needed

for riding or packing, were bunched together and driven by several boys.

Some Indian families were poor and had but one horse, while others had none. In either case, these people had to make the trip on foot. Old people who were poor were usually helped by other members of the tribe. Any family having more horses than they needed would lend a poor family a few horses for transporting their belongings.

The ideal travois horse was a large, heavily built, strong mare over four years old, although some Indians preferred a former saddle horse eight to nine years old. In the old buffalo days a horse was broken to haul a travois by tying a rawhide rope around its neck. To this rope long ropes were tied at each side and an old, dry buffalo hide tied to the ends. The horse was haltered and led by a man while one to three men or boys rode the hide.

As early as 1755, explorers, for want of a better word, described the Indians' carrying contrivance in their journals as a sled, and the French word *travois* did not come into use until much later. Most travois were constructed so that the shafts crossed over the neck of the horse, but some were made so that the shafts were placed on each side of the horse's body like those of a buggy.

One typical horse travois is the kind commonly used by the Blackfeet of Montana and Canada and is an enlarged copy of those pulled by dogs in the pre-horse days. The travois was made and owned by the women and was constructed solely of wood and rawhide.

The shafts (A – A) consisted of two pine poles, obtained along with the tepee poles from the eastern slopes of the Rockies, or the Bear Paw Mountains. The front projection forward of the tie (B) was made short so that the travois would ride well. The poles were crossed and tied together with a strip of sinew from the back of a buffalo's neck.

The hitch (C)—back of the tie—was a flat strip of rawhide about four fingers wide. The ends of this strip were passed under and around each shaft,

HORSE TRAVOIS

A, shafts; B, forward tie;
C, rawhide hitch; D, rawhide line;

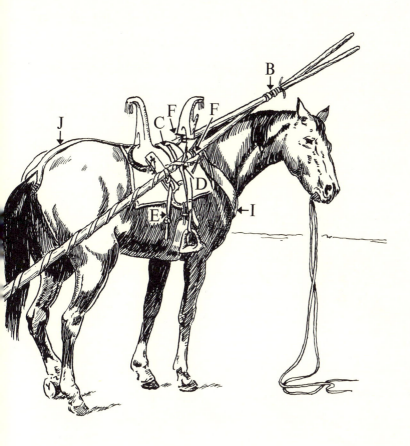

G.W. from EWERS

E, cinch; F, rawhide cord ties;
G, primary struts; H, secondary struts;
I, martingale; J, crooper

doubled back upon themselves, and sewed with rawhide strips. In the center of this strip two slits were cut crosswise, and through them was passed a long rawhide line about two fingers wide (D). One end of this line was wrapped tightly around each shaft down to the bottom edge of the loading platform. There the lines were tied, leaving the remaining part of each line free for use in tying the load to the platform.

The hitch included a cinch (E) of narrow rawhide rope. It was tied to one shaft, passed under the horse's belly, and tied to the shaft on the other side. The cinch was tied tight enough to hold the load, but without causing discomfort to the horse. Two rawhide cords (F – F) were wrapped around the shafts, forward of the hitch, and tied to the prongs of the saddle to secure the shafts.

The platform that carried the load consisted of two struts (G) placed across the shafts, about twenty inches apart. Notches were cut near the ends of the boards to fit over the shafts, where they were lashed in place by rawhide strips. Thinner struts (H) of birch or serviceberry were lashed about five inches apart beneath the cross struts. Quite often the bark was peeled from these struts, leaving evenly spaced bands of bark upon them for decorative purposes.

The platform was placed on the shafts so that the front end was about two feet from the horse's tail when the travois was in use. Either the wood saddle or the prairie-chicken-snare saddle was used on the travois horse with a martingale and crooper to hold the saddle in place. The martingale was a plain strip of rawhide three fingers wide, tied at each end of the pommel prongs (I). The crooper was also of rawhide, three fingers wide, with a padded tailpiece (J). Its forward portion passed under the rear horn of the saddle and tied to the prongs of the front horn.

At times a cage, made from bent willows, was added to the travois platform as a protection when carrying small children, old people, or puppy dogs too small to travel on their own. To keep out sun and rain, the willow framework was covered with a buffalo robe. Buffalo-skin sleeping robes and decorated willow backrests were carried on the travois, and some women placed the backrest on the travois platform in such a manner that the beaded hanger at the top of the backrest hung over the end of the platform, giving it an attractive appearance.

When not in actual use, the travois was either leaned against the outer wall of the tepee, or it was propped up, away from the lodge, with a third pole.

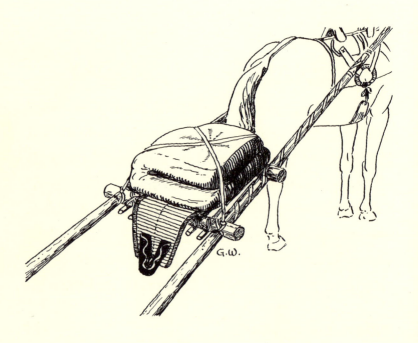

6 ▲ INDIAN TRAVEL TODAY

Today the manner in which the American Indian travels has been adapted a great deal to modern life. Still much of the equipment he uses would be familiar to his ancestors.

The Indians continue to use horses, not merely for recreation or display in parades, but in their daily work. Many Indians are ranchers, working either their own places or on tribal property, and their life is spent in the saddle. The Blackfeet and Cheyenne of Montana operate tribal ranches, and in Wyoming the Arapaho do the same. In their daily work with flocks of goats and sheep, the Navaho too still depend on the horse.

The horse is also all important to the Havasupais Indians of Arizona. Their home is located at the bottom of an extremely rugged section of the Grand Canyon, known as the Havasu Canyon. For centuries they have lived in this canyon 3,000 feet below the rim. The canyon floor averages only about one quarter mile in width, and there the Indians do their farming. Above the canyon floor they graze their livestock. Horses and mules are essential to them, for to reach their reservation they must travel an eight-mile-long trail down the side of the Grand Canyon, and no car can travel this rugged route.

The Indian dugout has nearly disappeared except among the Florida Seminoles where a few are still in use. Today, however, the new, fast airboat is rapidly taking its place. Also, the Cherokee of North Caro-

lina still make dugouts on their reservation. There the Indians have reconstructed one of their villages as it looked 200 years ago, and as one walks along the trails leading from cabins to craft shelters, one will come upon a clearing where some of the young Cherokee are burning and chipping out logs to show visitors how this work was done in earlier days.

The North Country Indians have forsaken their beautiful birchbark canoes in favor of canvas-covered canoes or sturdier craft made of modern materials. Still, the canoe, in either form, is much needed in the Indians' daily work. Guiding hunters and campers, hunting and fishing for their own food, and gathering wild rice are all jobs that depend upon the canoe. Today, however, when an Indian crosses a large lake in his canoe, the paddles rest on the floorboards while an outboard motor does the work.

In the northern regions snowshoes and sleds are still in use today. When the snows are deep across the land and through the forests, these age-old means of transportation are still the most reliable. Sled dogs, too, are still in service, although in some sections of the North the snowmobile is taking over.

To a limited extent the travois is being used here and there. It is still handy for hauling wood in places where neither car nor wagon can go. As late as 1904, records show that the Blackfeet Indians brought their travois into Browning, Montana, to haul food and supplies from the trading post, and it held a ceremonial place in the sun dance until about 1909.

Travois are made for display in the colorful parades at the Calgary Stampede and the Indian Days at Banff, both in Alberta, Canada. They also are seen at the Fourth of July celebration on the Blackfeet Reservation at Browning, Montana.

The automobile and the pickup truck, however, now take the place of the travois in most situations. When the Indians gather for special celebrations, they no longer ride the long miles on horseback, but come in cars, transporting their horses by truck or horse trailer.

*　*　*

Most of the younger generation of Indians are caught up in the hurried schedule of American life today. Although their lives are not so colorful now, they find modern ways of travel help them to accomplish more and enjoy more leisure time.

Nevertheless, the old Indians continue to move with the quiet dignity of the past. It is from these wise old men that we learn how their fathers and grandfathers lived and moved with the seasons as they followed the buffalo, the elk, and the moose. All too soon these men will make their last journey to the Sand Hills. May they have a good spirit horse under them as they ride along the Wolf Trail in the sky.

INDEX

*Indicates illustration

Robert Hofsinde was born in Denmark, where he received his formal education as well as his art training. In his late teens he came to the United States and settled in northern Minnesota. While trapping there one winter, he saved the life of a Chippewa Indian boy, and in gratitude the Chippewa made him a blood brother of the tribe, giving him the name Gray-Wolf. This contact led him to a profound interest in the culture of the Indian, and in the years that followed he engaged in comprehensive research among many different tribes. Today he is a recognized authority in the field. An author of many books on Indian lore, he is often asked to give lectures and to make TV appearances. He and his wife live in Orange County, New York.